COMMON GROUND

COMMON GROUND

A.J. PRETORIUS

SIMON GUY

Fast Foot Press
Lancaster

CONTENTS

INTRODUCTION: FRAMING THE IMAGES

Common Ground has emerged from a collaborative conversation between a photographer, A.J. Pretorius and a writer, Simon Guy, with the book curated in dialogue with a graphic designer, Simon Hawkesworth.

The conversation started with the photographs in this book, which were taken on three sites in late 2015/early 2016. The first site is a community centre, where a series of portraits were made to explore how the facility enables a shared social dynamic. The second site, a plot of scrubland wedged between disused industrial buildings, a football pitch, and wetlands, had served as a shared public space for generations before it was fenced off. The "no trespassing" notices on its periphery were photographed to collate and compare how they had been vandalised as acts of protest. For the third site, the fields bordering the community centre were photographed. Here, local government had appealed against the land's protected status as a measure to restrict public access to a nearby school playground and the images comment on the polarising effect of this move on local opinion.

These images stimulated a conversation between A.J. Pretorius and Simon Guy about the way photography can serve to catalyse public debate about the contested meanings and experiences of spaces, places and communities, at a time of intense political change. The result was the textual interventions that frame the photographs in this book, which offer a narrative framework that allows Common Ground to raise and explore the tensions, contradictions, and questions that result from different claims to shared physical and social space.

The book has been designed to avoid fixed meanings and to encourage reflection and dialogue. Interleaving images, an essay, quotations and a structured dialogue, the book aims to invite and perhaps even provoke responses. Readers may follow the narrative order or dip into the content as they desire. By revealing and reflecting on issues of land acquisition and management, our shared intent is to catalyse a public conversation around what is so often a private practice, the experience of place.

PORTRAITS/SIGNS

Nothing is less real than realism. Details are confusing. It is only by selection, by elimination, by emphasis, that we get at the real meaning of things.

Georgia O'Keefe, 1922.

An instant photographed can only acquire meaning insofar as the viewer can read into it a duration extending beyond itself. When we find a photograph meaningful, we are lending it a past and a future.

John Berger, 1982.

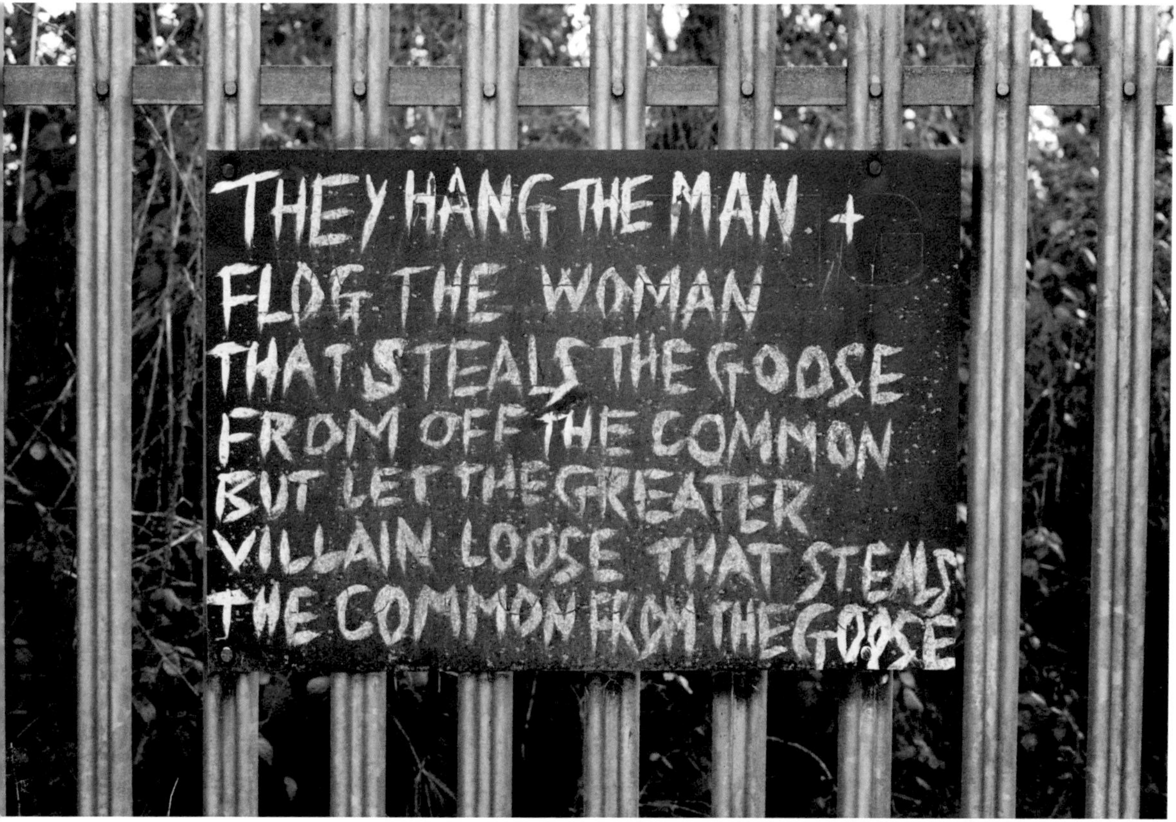
THEY HANG THE MAN +
FLOG THE WOMAN
THAT STEALS THE GOOSE
FROM OFF THE COMMON
BUT LET THE GREATER
VILLAIN LOOSE THAT STEALS
THE COMMON FROM THE GOOSE

ESSAY: ANOTHER WAY OF ASKING

The writer and critic John Berger famously made a distinction between a public and a private use of photography; the one rendering the subject "mute", the other providing a "meeting place for diverse remembered experiences which, in one way or another, across time and space, are tangential to the moment recorded". This is what he describes as *Another Way of Telling*, a photographic practice that allows for the subject to "constitute" as well as being "constituted". For Berger, what suggests the distinctness of private photography is its intentionality; rather than being a mere fragment taken from the world as public photographs tend to be, private photographs can serve as a referent to the world. Less a source of isolated information, which is the function of most public photographs, private photographs, in connection with personal memory, may suggest multiple references and produce meaning. Berger here connects with a view of the redemptive potential of photography that we find strongly in the writing of Walter Benjamin, specifically in his essay, *A Short History of Photography*:

> However skilful the photographer, however carefully he poses his model, the spectator feels a compulsion to look for the tiny spark of chance, of the here and now, with which reality has, as it were, seared the character in the picture; to find that imperceptible point at which, in the immediacy of that long past moment, the future so persuasively inserts itself that, looking back, we may discover it. It is indeed a different nature that speaks to the camera from the one which addresses the eye…

According to Benjamin this "spark of chance" is related to our memory through what he terms the "optical unconscious", "which photography makes us aware of for the first time". Like Berger, Benjamin is critical of the part played by photography in the development of a commodified culture, but shares his belief in the productive power of photography, a power to disrupt the "sense of sameness of things in the world", or in Berger's terms, to make a subjective reference that opposes the abstraction of reification. Key to this other *way of seeing* is the central ambiguity of the photographic image, which is always "irrefutable as evidence but weak in meaning". It is this photographic ambiguity that for Berger offers to photography a "unique means of expression", and a "possible theory of photography".

There are strong echoes here of the more recent debates around critical realism in the photography of Allan Sekula, who used photographs to comment and invite debate around the local effects of globalisation and the emergence of post-industrial economies. Sekula employed textual and photographic assemblages that draw on the power of images to locate the spectator in space and time, but at the same time disrupt any desire to equate photographic accuracy with historical or political objectivity. Sekula wanted to move away from any idea of documentary photography as a window on the world, while also avoiding the aestheticisation of the social, risked by framing photographs as art objects distant from reality. Instead, he sought to balance documentary and art in a photographic practice that, according to Jan Baetens and Hilde Van Gelder, sought to "understand social reality by critically making notes of it…through inscriptions and traces of the reality that surrounds us". The aim of this photographic method is to raise questions without providing a readymade answer, to leave "traces in our mind" in order to encourage "reflection". The political intent here is not to enflame sudden passion and collective political awakening, but rather to encourage a slower process of individual engagement, which in turn may effect cultural change.

Common Ground follows a similar photographic method, drawing upon qualities of photographic ambiguity to open up space for dialogue, interpretation and potential disruption. For while each image works individually, intriguing in their own way, possessing their own possible stories and singular interpretations, it is the juxtaposition of images that is productive. On the left we find a series of portraits, not quite formally posed but certainly not spontaneous. This is not candid photography in the tradition of Henri Cartier-Bresson, who famously spoke of the *decisive moment* in which the photographer could *pounce* to *trap life* in an instant. In candid photography, the photographer is in control, the subject passive, the moment defined by the framing and timing of the person in charge of the shutter release. In this collection, Pretorius takes a different path, with a knowing and empathetic relationship established between photographer and subject.

One can imagine a conversation preceding the capture of the image. Who are you and what are your intentions? Why are you taking these photographs here and why do you want to photograph me? A rapport established, the subjects are drawn into the photo shoot and adopt their chosen pose and expression, not quite relaxed, but not quite formal. This is an unexpected event, but not artificial and each subject appears to feel some control over their image. This is who I am, at least in this moment. We almost feel we could know these individuals, and maybe some viewers will? But in the end the ambiguity remains.

And then moving our eyes across to the right page, to the images of the warning signs, each is altered both by natural processes of decay, but also by human intervention. These are absent portraits, expressions of unknown people with uncertain motivations. But they existed, they have a left an intentional mark on this landscape, which Pretorius recognises and captures. He has chosen the time and the frame, but the expression of the individual remains clear, though of course still ambiguous.

In opening the book and looking left then right and then back again, we are faced with a double ambiguity, which seems to offer some meaning – a possible semantic resolution? Was it those in the portraits who defaced the signs? Maybe not. But then, if not, who? What are the stories here, are the motivations all the same, is it a campaign, or is it random? Of course, Pretorius has chosen the layout and possibly we feel we can read his intent, but we cannot be sure.

What is significant is that there is no attempt by the photographer to fix the meaning, no titles or captions to explain or encourage a particular view of each image. Rather there is an invitation to make connections, to join a debate, to express a view. These are not photographs simply for silent contemplation or aesthetic pleasure, even if we do find the images visually pleasing. Instead what they ask for is a response, an expression, an opinion. These images say there is something in the relationship between these people and this landscape that needs to be surfaced, illuminated and expressed. These photographs do not offer "matters of fact", they present "matters of concern", as the sociologist Bruno Latour would put it. Or put another, John Berger way, these "photographs do not translate from appearances. They quote from them".

Perhaps it is only in the final three frames, presented in series, in which we might more firmly pinpoint the photographer's intentions: the lady and dog walking freely over (presumably) common ground, the wire fencing covered with blossom, and finally the firmly locked gate – cold, grey and definitively locked. Here we might sense a position, a narrative of freedom and constraint of movement. Through these images the photographer asks, do you recognise my concerns, do you share them?

So returning to Berger's distinction, this collection is paradoxically better viewed as private photography, rather than public. Collecting these images together does not represent a fixed ideological or political statement, a manifesto. Instead we are offered visual traces, provocations which act as a catalyst to spur debate about what connects us to each other as communities and to the physical and mental landscapes we inhabit, individually and collectively. Photography alone cannot do much more given its ambiguous nature. But by celebrating this ambiguity *Common Ground* avoids simply using photography to voice prescribed views and instead invites viewers of the collection to respond by voicing theirs. These images are asking **what do you think?**

LANDSCAPES

The question was never to get away from facts but closer to them, not fighting empiricism but, on the contrary, renewing empiricism…[T]he critical mind, if it is to renew itself and be relevant again, is to be found in the cultivation of a stubbornly realist attitude - to speak like William James - but a realism dealing with what I will call matters of concern, not matters of fact.

Bruno Latour, 2004.

In other words, the photograph, as it stands alone, presents merely the possibility of meaning.

Allan Sekula, 1984.

DIALOGUE: CONCERNING PHOTOGRAPHY

In this structured dialogue between photographer and writer, key themes running through the project are highlighted and explored.

INTENT

Simon Guy (SG): This book can be seen as motivated by a number of concerns: the relationship between people and place; the question of access to land as a public space; ideas of identity and community in a period of neo-nationalism; questions of truth and "post-truth"; and the role of photographs in illustrating these issues, and so on. As Bruno Latour suggests, these concerns are the result of our entanglement in a world in which truth or "facts" struggle to explain our experiences. How, we wanted to ask, can creative practices such as photography and critical writing act to surface these matters of concern?

A.J. Pretorius (AJP): To provide some historical context, this work was undertaken in the run-up to, and aftermath of Britain's referendum on EU membership. Like many recent socio-political developments, this was characterised by a discourse appealing to emotional reactions rather than critical analysis. As a response to such scenarios, the intent of this work is to provoke critical reflection. In terms of the work itself, photography easily resorts to mere representation, and a combination of image and text easily resorts to mere repetition in two representational modes. This book intends to develop an integrated approach where there is productive interaction between different photographs, between photographs and text, and between different texts themselves.

PRACTICE

AJP: The three sites that were photographed for this book were approached in different ways. For the first, the set of posed portraits required engaging with the subjects, explaining the work's objective, and acquiring subjects' consent. For the second site, a systematic photographic inventory was made, while a more traditional documentary approach was taken for the third site. The similar frontal perspective of the posed portraits and the photographs of the "no trespassing" notices allows these to be presented as a series of diptychs. This leads to a productive interaction between photographs - with the aim of engaging the viewer - that would be absent if they were presented apart. This, in turn, contrasts with the sequence of three landscapes that is presented in a way that is more traditional and perhaps narrower in symbolism. An important part of this work was to acknowledge the limited ability of the three sets of photographs, if presented in isolation, to explore larger themes. Through dialogue with the writer, a strategy was developed where image and text are interleaved and where neither is privileged over the other. Some contextual framing is provided, but the objective is to strike a balance between being prescriptive and allowing for open-ended interpretation.

SG: It is customary in books about photography (and art more generally) for the writer to provide a commentary, sometimes critical, often flattering, to "flesh out" the book, to give it "authority" perhaps by providing a context, often around the place of the images in the canonical history of photography. The purpose here is different, not simply to tease out meaning or explain the content of the images, but rather to expand the space of interpretation. Some other writers are cited, not just for the purpose of lending authority to this author's claims, but rather to provide further intellectual resources that might widen the field of understanding.

COLLABORATION

SG: If we are truly living in a post-disciplinary world of deepening complexity, then we must respond by assembling and exploring different creative practices that, taken together and in dialogue, might help to make sense of the world in which we are implicated. While the intertwined practices of photography and writing have been periodically explored, it is always presented as an "innovation", a novelty to be experienced as something apart from the mainstream of photographic art practice we see in museums and galleries.

AJP: In the 1960s, Marshall McLuhan wrote of the tendency of a medium itself to assume the role of message. Moreover, by privileging the photograph through a process of aestheticisation, there arises the risk of completely formalising meaning, as critics like Martha Rosler have argued. Collaboration offers an opportunity to counter this. Through a strategy of combining different competences and different modes of content, collaboration can instil a work with depth in more than one dimension, like photography and writing in the case of this book. At the same time, an interesting dynamic arises when it is conceded that a medium of choice, like photography, is limited in what it can achieve, and that this deficit can not only be compensated for by collaboration, but that the final outcome has the potential of raising questions that would otherwise remain unasked.

DIALOGUE

SG: The book could read in a number of ways, linearly, as it is presented by the authors, or in any other way. By presenting the text and images in this way we are inviting multiple readings to stimulate a response from the reader and to encourage a conversation, even a debate.

AJP: The notion of dialogue, or exchange, is important and present at different levels in this book: between collaborators, between the different elements of the work, and between the work and the reader/viewer. It has already been noted how the dialogue between the collaborators was instrumental in conceiving and producing this book. In terms of an exchange with the reader/viewer, the objective is to invite them to engage with the work from their own point of departure, with reference to their own ideological, social, and historical baggage, so to speak. To avoid being so open-ended as to be meaningless, the exchange between the different photographic and textual elements are important to anchor and guide possible avenues of deduction.

IMPACT

AJP: There is a somewhat subversive element to this work: it aims to undermine both indifference and conceitedness. To have impact, it will interrupt or suspend existing patterns of thought, lead to questions, and ideally to discussion. In this way, the book aims to explore the tensions, contradictions, and questions raised by (possibly conflicting) claims to shared material, social, and ideological spaces.

SG: If we can encourage the book to be picked up, glanced through, read, passed around and discussed then we will have achieved our aims. The idea is not to proselytise and convert to a particular political position but to catalyse reflection and debate during a period which has been often described as "post-truth".

SOURCES

Jan Baetens and Hilde Van Gelder, *Critical Realism in Contemporary Art*, Leuven University Press, 2010.

Tanya Barson, *Georgia O'Keefe*, Tate Publishing, 2016 (original Georgia O'Keefe quote 1922).

Walter Benjamin, "A Short History of Photography" (originally published 1931), In *On Photography*, Reaction Books, 2015.

John Berger and Jean Mohr, *Another Way of Telling: A Possible Theory of Photography*, Bloomsbury Publishing, 2016 (originally published 1982).

Henri Cartier-Bresson, "The Decisive Moment", In *The Minds Eye*, *Writings on Photography and Photographers*, Aperture, 2014 (originally published in *Images à la Sauvette (Images On the Run)*, 1952).

Bruno Latour, "Why Has Critique Run out of Steam? From Matters of Fact to Matters of Concern", *Critical Inquiry* 30, no. 2, 2004.

Marshall McLuhan, "The medium is the message", In *Understanding Media: The Extensions of Man*, Routledge, 2001 (originally published 1964).

Martha Rosler, "In, around, and afterthoughts (on documentary photography)" (originally published 1981), In *Decoys and Disruptions: Selected Writings, 1975–2001*, MIT Press, 2004.

Allan Sekula, *Photography Against the Grain: Essays and Photos Works, 1973–1983*, Press of the Nova Scotia College of Art and Design, 1984.

BIOGRAPHIES

A.J. PRETORIUS

A.J. Pretorius is a photographer whose work to date has examined the interaction between material conditions and social context. In a previous book, *Unhome*, he explored immigration from a personal perspective by photographically commenting on the state of suspension between familiar and foreign. Before he turned to photography, he worked at the intersection of computer science and visual design, and was awarded a Leverhulme Fellowship for his research on data visualisation.

SIMON GUY

Simon Guy is Professor of Design and Society at Lancaster University. His research explores the co-evolution of art, design and development in the pursuit of sustainable urban futures. His work is interdisciplinary and collaborative, most recently working with sculptor Wolfgang Weileder on an Arts and Humanities Research Council project, *Jetty*, which explored the role of public art in generating public debate about urban sustainability, and led to the publication of *Catalyst: Art, Sustainability and Place in the work of Wolfgang Weileder*, Bielefeld/New York: Kerber Verlag.

SIMON HAWKESWORTH

Simon Hawkesworth has worked in higher education for over twenty-five years, working in learning development, research and teaching, as well as developing a private design and publishing practice, Fast Foot Press. His research interests include: architectural lettering, printed ephemera and Modernist design. Recent publications have been: *A Lancaster Alphabet*, *A Lancaster Ephemera*, and *The Winton Murder*, co-authored with Michael Murphy.

Common Ground by A.J. Pretorius & Simon Guy.

First published in Great Britain in 2017 by Fast Foot Press.

British Library Cataloguing in Publication Data. A catalogue record for this book is available from the British Library.

ISBN: 978-0-9571922-6-3

Printed by Wallace Printers of Bolton, Lancashire, using Conqueror stock. Set in Janson, DIN 1451 and Whitney typefaces.

Fast Foot Press is an independent publisher and design studio. Based in Lancaster, it develops publications relating to social history, architecture, the arts and design.

Fast Foot Press

18 Hastings Road, Lancaster, LA1 4TH, UK

w: www.fastfootpress.co.uk — e: info@fastfootpress.co.uk